Identity

Mini Jane Johnston

ZONDERVAN
PUBLISHING HOUSE
OF THE ZONDERVAN CORPORATION
GRAND RAPIDS, MICHIGAN 49506

This book is composed of the following:
REAL IDENTITY, DIRECTION, MOTIVATION, and SPIRITUAL FITNESS

Library of Congress Catalog Card Number: 73-15045

Contents

To
the friend
—the professor—
and all those along the way
who have cared and shared

Real Identity

6

Who am I
in this maze of life?
A statistic
on a commissioner's report?
A name on a list
arranged alphabetically?
Or a number
in some computer?
Or a self-owned will
living for ego?
Is life so empty?
Do I just fill space?
I want to know—
I've got to know.
God created me for a purpose,
and He loves me.
He showed me His love
in dying for me.
He wants my love in return.
Then life has a meaning.

Ruth Graham Dienert

It was morning . . . I had come alive . . .
 on the inside, that is.

Something was different . . .
 life had new meaning.
 I had found reality!

It all began with my search for *identity*
 and the answer to the mysterious question,
 Who am I?

A friend had asked me directly one day,
 "Have you ever read what God says about it?"

"What God says?" I answered with surprise.
 "Where in the world would I find what
 God says about my identity?"

"In the first book of the Bible," he replied.

Never having owned a Bible,
and not wishing to display my ignorance,
I was about to change the subject when
my friend offered to read the suggested answer.

I listened with interest and heard for the first time
the Genesis account of man:

 "And the Lord God formed man of the
 dust of the ground, and breathed (from
 Himself) into his nostrils the breath of

life; and man became a living soul. So
God created man in his own image, in
the image of God created he them."[1]

My friend told me that when God created man,
He gave him immediate relationship and conver-
sation with Himself. He wanted someone on
earth whom He could love and who would love
Him in return.

As God and man walked together in mutual love
and enjoyment, their friendship was beautiful.

In perfect harmony and kinship with God,
man had a complete sense of belonging,
thereby knowing his own identity.

"God made man a responsible being with freedom of choice and placed him in an ideal en-
vironment," my friend continued.

"In response, man was to show that he loved
God by obeying a simple command,

" 'Do not eat from this tree or you will
certainly die.' "[2]

---

[1] Gen. 2:7; 1:27 (*King James Version*).

[2] "The test could have been something else. No act of
primitive magic is involved here. This is the infinite-personal
God calling on personal man to act by choice. . . . He could
so act by choice because he was created to be different
from the animal, the plant and the machine. . ." Francis A.
Schaeffer, *The God Who Is There* (p. 104).

Sensing that I was completely uninformed, my
    friend explained . . .
    this was not a kill-joy God saying "No! No!"
    and withholding something good.

It was the same loving God giving man
    moral guidelines,
    based on His own character,
    which would preserve for man the very
    life God had given to him.

"We seem to be a far cry from that utopian
ideal today," I commented. "Whatever happened?"

"Unbelievable as it may seem," he continued,
"there came a day when man believed Satan's lie:

    " 'You won't die at all; but rather you'll
    become like God yourself, with expanded
    knowledge and experience.'

"Although God had said that disobedience
would bring death, man doubted God's Word,
challenged His authority, and turned willfully to
his own way.

"Something catastrophic happened when man
took that fatal step! His nature changed when
disobedience and pride became a part of his being. He destroyed personal companionship with
a holy God by his own choice. The Bible is clear:

" 'When Adam sinned, sin entered the entire human race. His sin spread [physical and spiritual] death throughout all the world, so everything began to grow old and die, for all sinned.' "[3]

"Well, this is the first time I ever realized why we all die when God made us to live," I interrupted.

"Yes, God and sin cannot live together," my friend continued. "Man was suddenly estranged and fallen from his Sovereign Center and knew for the first time

> fear
> guilt[4]
> and lostness.

"Instead of being God-centered,
> he became self-centered,
> turning to himself for
> satisfaction
> wisdom
> and guidance.

---

[3] Rom. 5:12 *(Living Bible)*.

[4] "Whoever sins is guilty of breaking God's law, for every sin is done against the will of God" (1 John 3:4, *Good News for Modern Man; Living Bible*).

"This self-centeredness and separation from God led mankind into universal problems of
aloneness
hopelessness
and despair.

"He was unable to recapture the spiritual and physical life that God had given to him. He feared death."

"But aren't you forgetting man's other side? Look at his accomplishments!"

"It's true," he explained. "Man is a contradiction. One moment he does that which is noble and praiseworthy,
but the next . . .
that which is base and vile.
Sometimes he seems akin to God.
Other times he acts like the devil.

"Sin has become a part of man and marred the Creator's original handiwork."

"That's a pretty depressing picture," I commented. "I need more encouragement than that."

"We all do," he laughed, "and that's why we have Christmas."

"Christmas?" I queried. "How does Christmas relate to this?"

"Well, Christmas was the time that God proved how much He loves us by giving His Son as the

14

only possible way out of our impasse. We find in Matthew 1:20-21:

> " '. . . the child within her [Mary] has been conceived by the Holy Spirit. And she will have a Son, and you shall name him Jesus (meaning Savior), for he will save his people from their sins' " *(Living Bible).*

"That rings a bell," I interjected. "I remember that from the *Messiah.*"

"Yes, He was born on earth so man could see God in a human body and talk with Him personally. Jesus Christ compassionately identified with man by entering into
his aloneness
his joys
and his sorrows.

"The Savior's endless, unchanging love for man reached an awesome climax when

> " '. . . Christ willingly gave himself to God to die for our sins. . . .'[5]

"That's why we call the day of His crucifixion Good Friday—
'good' for us
because God's Son was crucified on the cross as our substitute."

---

5 Heb. 9:14 *(Ibid.).*

"In reality Jesus was saying: 'Father, let Me take the punishment and death for their disobedience.' In that dark hour the blackness of our iniquity agonized the soul of the Savior as

" 'God laid on him the guilt and sins of every one of us.'[6]

"It is finished!" Jesus cried out in solitary triumph. He had paid the penalty for our transgressions.

"Now, a holy God can justly pardon and reconcile to Himself anyone who puts his faith in Jesus Christ."

"Is that the real meaning of Good Friday?" I asked.

"Yes, it is," my friend responded as he turned to another part of his Bible.

" 'For he [God] has rescued us out of the darkness and gloom of Satan's kingdom and brought us into the kingdom of his dear

---

[6] Isa. 53:6 (*Living Bible*).

Son, who bought our freedom with his blood and forgave us all our sins.'[7]

"And that's what removes our guilt," my friend said with assurance.

"Removes guilt?" I questioned. "How?"

---

[7] Col. 1:13-14. *(Ibid.).*

Painting © 1967 by Marjorie Nordwell

" 'Come, let's talk this over, says the Lord;
no matter how deep the stain of your sins,
I can take it out and make you as clean as
freshly fallen snow. . . .'[8]

" 'The power of the blood of Christ . . . will
cleanse our conscience from . . . our former
ways. . . .'[9]

"When you believe these promises and ask
God to forgive you, He absolves your personal
guilt."

"Seems unbelievable that it's all so simple," I
reasoned.

"You can't really say it's simple or easy—it's
costly! True, it's simple by faith to accept His
forgiveness, however—
we must be willing in love
to give ourselves to Christ
to obey His Word
to give heart allegiance to a new way of Life.

"This may involve struggle and sacrifice as we
relinquish our lives to Him; but it all seems small
and insignificant in comparison with His sacrifi-
cial love for us.

---

[8] Isa. 1:18 (*Ibid.*).
[9] Heb. 9:14 (*New English Bible*).

" 'For the free gift of eternal salvation
is now being offered to everyone; and
along with this gift comes the realiza-
tion that God wants us to turn from god-
less living and sinful pleasures and to
live good, God-centered lives day after
day, looking forward to the happy fulfillment of our hope when . . . our . . . Saviour
Christ Jesus will appear.' "[10]

"You seem to imply that He loves everyone."

"It's true," he responded. "Christ's love has no
favorites. He loves and accepts us just the way
we are."

"Aren't you ever afraid that someday this model
theory might all come crashing down around
you?" I questioned.

"It would have come crashing down long ago
had it depended on me. But it all depends on
the miraculous resurrection of Jesus Christ—cele-
brated each year at Easter."

"Easter," I reflected. "Guess it's more the tra-
ditional with me—
    colored eggs
    a family holiday
    and a smart new outfit."

---

[10] Titus 2:11-12 *(Living Bible)*; v. 13 *(New English Bible)*.

"There's more to it than that," my friend continued with an amused glint in his eyes. "Easter was the day that Jesus Christ came back to life

Photo by John P. Malick

again just as He said He would:

" 'And by being raised from the dead
he was proved to be the mighty Son of
God. . . .'[11]

"He conquered death—and affirmed to the
world:

" 'I am the resurrection and the life.
Anyone who believes in me, even
though he dies like anyone else,
shall live again. He is given
eternal life for believing in me
and shall never perish.'
(John 11:25-26. *King James Version;
Living Bible*).

"Before going back to heaven to be our mediator before God,[12] Jesus promised His disciples:

" 'I will send the Holy Spirit . . .
to live in you
to counsel you
to comfort you
to fill you with power.'[13]

---

[11] Rom. 1:4 *(Living Bible)*.

[12] "For there is one God, and one mediator between God
and men, the man Christ Jesus . . . (who) returned trium-
phantly to heaven after his resurrection and victory over
Satan . . ." (1 Tim. 2:5, *King James Version;* Eph. 4:8, *Living
Bible*).

[13] "But the Counselor, the Holy Spirit, whom the Father
will send in my name, he will teach you all things . . ." (John
14:26, *Revised Standard Version*).

" 'He will lead you into all truth and
will never leave you.'[14]

"Christ was saying to them: Although my bodily presence will be removed, through the Holy
Spirit I will be united with you in a more inti-
mate oneness than we have ever known. You
will never be alone!"

"But how can something which happened two
thousand years ago possibly affect me now?" I
asked doubtfully.

"Because Jesus is alive and in the *now!*

"He has a revolutionary effect in us today if
we're willing to be made new and come God's
way."

"What do you mean, 'Come God's way'?" I asked.

"It means to change your mind and attitude
about God
    to see yourself a sinner needing a Savior
    to turn from your rebellion and indifference
    to ask His forgiveness
    to accept His life-giving proposal."[15]

"Proposal?"

---

[14] Luke 24:49; John 14:15-17; 15-26 *(author's paraphrase)*.
[15] John 11:25-26 *(King James Version; Living Bible)*.

"Yes," he continued, "Christ states it this way:

" 'Look! I have been standing at the door
and I am constantly knocking. If anyone
hears me calling him and opens the door,
I will come in and fellowship with him
and he with me.'[16]

"This simply means that Jesus Christ is knocking at the door of your life. If you will open the door, He will come into you in the Person of the Holy Spirit.

"His living presence within you breaks the power of sin and self; He restores the relationship that man first enjoyed with God and then forfeited.

"Now, what is your response to Christ?
Will you be indifferent to His knocking?
Or will you respond to His love and
invite Him into your life?"[17]

"I've never really thought about it seriously, I guess. In fact, you're the first person who ever took the time to explain it to me.

I'll think about it," I answered.

In a gracious way, my friend further informed me

---

[16] Rev. 3:20 *(Living Bible)*.

[17] "God is using us to speak to you . . . as though Christ himself were here . . . appealing direct to you . . . receive the love he offers you—be reconciled to God" (2 Cor. 5:20, *Phillips, Living Bible*).

23

that, if I realized that Jesus Christ came to deliver me from my inherited sinful nature and, realizing this, refused to let Him do so, then I would personally choose the penalty of rejection.[18]

Turning again in the Bible, he read:

"Someday we're all going to face the Father's supreme court. Yes, each of us will give an account of himself to God. He's the one we have to answer to."[19]

" 'Think how much more terrible the punishment will be for those who have trampled underfoot the Son of God and treated his cleansing blood as though it were common and unhallowed, and insulted and outraged the Holy Spirit who brings God's mercy to his people.'[20]

" 'They will be punished in everlasting hell, forever separated from the face of the Lord, never to see the glory of his power.'

" 'The Lord . . . is patient toward you,' " my friend added, " 'not wishing for any to perish but for all to come to repentance.'[21]

"But, of course, it's your choice.
You decide . . .
you alone."

---

[18] Jude 14, 15 *(Living Bible)*.
[19] Rom. 14:10-12 *(Letters to Street Christians, Living Bible)*.
[20] Heb. 10:29; 2 Thess. 1:9 *(Living Bible)*.
[21] 2 Pet. 3:9 *(New American Standard Bible)*.

So it was that soon afterward,
   while realizing my own emptiness
   and the wonder of God's personal love
   in Christ,

I simply said,
   "Lord, I never knew before that You
      suffered and died so that I could be forgiven.
   I never knew You loved me as a person
      and wanted to come into my life.
   I didn't know I was keeping You on the
      outside. I'm sorry.
   The door's open—
      Come in."
I waited . . .
   but nothing seemed to happen.
   No lights flashed.
   I didn't see stars or hear bells.

Unfortunately, as I looked in the mirror,
   there was no improvement.

"Guess I'm a reject," I reasoned.
   "Maybe God is fussy—
   and He well might be!
   I've pretty much ignored Him up to this point.
"And maybe . . .
   maybe He isn't there after all!"
However, before crawling into bed I quietly
mumbled the only prayer I ever knew.
   "Now I lay me down to sleep. . . ."

The next morning when I awakened . . .
  something did seem different!
Do you know what it was?
  For the first time in my life, I felt
  like saying "Good morning" to God.
Before, I had always jumped out of bed
  grabbed life by the tail
  and started ordering it around.
Now it seemed easy,
  almost natural,
  to think
  "Lord, what do You have in mind when You
    think of me today?"

I was aware of God.
  There was simple communication.
  I had come alive spiritually![22]

I felt a new peace within me . . .
  and a warm sense of *belonging* to God.[23]

---

[22] "(Jesus said), Men can only reproduce human life, but the Holy Spirit gives new life from heaven; so don't be surprised at my statement that you must be born again (spiritually)!" (John 3:6-7, *Living Bible*).

[23] "He has . . . given us his Holy Spirit in our hearts as guarantee that we *belong to him.* . . . And we . . . have been baptized into a spiritual union and communion with Christ, the Messiah. . . . Now you . . . *belong* in God's [family] with every other Christian" (2 Cor. 1:22; Gal. 3:26-27; Eph. 2:19, *Amplified, Living Bible*).

There was a certain air of joy and expectancy,
   a certain newness,
   like having a new person on the inside.

As the Bible says:

   "When someone becomes a Christian
   he becomes a brand new person inside.

   He is not the same any more. A new
   life has begun!"[24]

Finally, I had met the God I had always wanted to love and thank for creation and being. I was beginning to identify with my Creator-Friend.

I was no longer a stranger to myself.[25]
I had found my *real identity!*

Thanks to my friend who told me how to find it.

He cared!

---

[24] 2 Cor. 5:17 *(Ibid.)*.

[25] "We've got the Spirit inside to tell us who we are . . . and he does" (1 Cor. 2:10; Rom. 8:23, *Letters to Street Christians*).

Come Alive!

Words and Music by
DOROTHY JEAN BUTLER

Direction

Where am I going?
Does life have a plan
with direction and fulfillment?
Or is life just vague chance—
trial and error,
cause and effect?
Can I know,
as the Bible says,
that my steps are directed
by the Lord?*
Can He be trusted as a Guide
to tell the truth,
to show the way?
Does He have a source
of guidance
which gives the answers?
How can I be sure?
It's so very important,
for I will not pass
this way again.

M. J. J.

Psalm 37:23 (Living Bible).

Where can I find *direction* for life?

Often I pondered this question in college.

> Am I taking the right courses?
> Will I end up like a multitude of others,
>   unhappy in what I am doing,
>   with no real goal or purpose?

It was rather scary at times!

Then I met a professor who wasn't afraid to talk about God and who communicated the answer.
> "Do you know that God has a blueprint for your life?" she asked me one day.

"Oh, I'm not sure," I answered. "I guess God helps those who help themselves."

> "He can do better than that," she quickly responded. "He can help you more than you can help yourself.
>   "Have you ever read Psalm 32:8?"

"No, I have not," I answered. "I'm just beginning to know there is an Old and New Testament."

> "Read it," she suggested. "It's a great statement on direction!"

A Student's Prayer

John W. Peterson

Possibly from W. A. Mozart

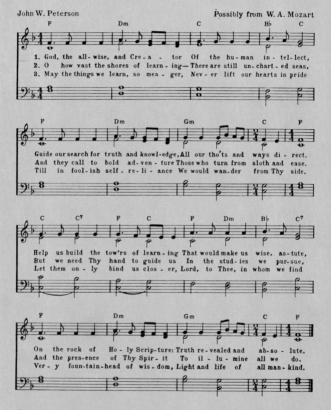

1. God, the all-wise, and Cre-a-tor Of the hu-man in-tel-lect,
Guide our search for truth and knowl-edge, All our tho'ts and ways di-rect.
Help us build the tow'rs of learn-ing That would make us wise, as-tute,
On the rock of Ho-ly Scrip-ture: Truth re-vealed and ab-so-lute.

2. O how vast the shores of learn-ing—There are still un-chart-ed seas,
And they call to bold ad-ven-ture Those who turn from sloth and ease.
But we need Thy hand to guide us In the stud-ies we pur-sue,
And the pres-ence of Thy Spir-it To il-lu-mine all we do.

3. May the things we learn, so mea-ger, Nev-er lift our hearts in pride
Till in fool-ish self-re-li-ance We would wan-der from Thy side.
Let them on-ly bind us clos-er, Lord, to Thee, in whom we find
Ver-y foun-tain-head of wis-dom, Light and life of all man-kind.

" 'I, the Lord, will instruct you and teach
you in the way you should go; I will counsel
you with My eye upon you.' "[1]
"Doesn't that sound as if God has a plan
for your life? What do you think it means?"

Slowly, I read it again.

" 'I, **the Lord,** will instruct **you** and teach
you in the way **you** should go. I
will counsel **you** with My eye upon
you.'

"Why, yes, it does seem personal. It repeats
you five times in that one statement. He must
want to give me direction.

"But where do I find His instructions?
Are they hard to understand?" I asked.

"No, they aren't," she answered. "This handbook
for life, the Bible, gives us the guidelines needed
for direction and fulfillment—
but you must take the time to read them!

"God wouldn't have instructions so essential for
your life and then make them difficult to understand. He is too loving and available for that.

" 'The whole Bible was given to us by
inspiration from God and is useful to teach
us what is true and to make us realize what

[1] Ps. 32:8 *(Amplified Bible).*

is wrong in our lives. . . . It is God's way
of making us well prepared at every point,
fully equipped to do good to everyone."[2]

"Guidance," she continued, "comes by knowing
what the Bible says to do and then doing it.
In it we read:

> " 'I am but a pilgrim here on earth:
> how I need a map—
> and your commands are my chart and guide.
> You will keep on guiding me all my life
> with your wisdom and counsel. . . .
> Happy are all who follow (Your)
> instructions.'[3]

"God's written instructions are interpreted to you
by the Holy Spirit
   so you can understand
   and follow them.

"The Holy Spirit is a Person
   with infinite intellect
   will
   and emotion.[4]

---

[2] 2 Tim. 3:16-17 (*Living Bible*).

[3] Pss. 119:19; 73:24; Prov. 8:13 (*Ibid.*).

[4] William R. Bright, *The Christian and the Holy Spirit*,
Campus Crusade for Christ, International, p. 9.

Intellect: "No one can know God's thoughts except God's
own Spirit" (1 Cor. 2:11, *Ibid.*).

Will: "It is the same and only Holy Spirit who gives all . . .

"He is God living in your humanity.

"When you first believed in Jesus Christ and received Him as your Savior,"[5] the professor continued, "the Holy Spirit came to take up residence in your body.

> " 'Haven't you yet learned that your body is the home of the Holy Spirit God gave you[6] and that he lives within you?'

"Before the Spirit of God entered your life," she explained, "your human nature dominated you.

"For instance, we watch a baby's tricks with delight, but soon we see that he wants to be the center of attention and is unhappy and frustrated when he is thwarted and cannot have his own way.

---

gifts and powers, deciding which each one of us should have" (1 Cor. 12:11, *Ibid.*).
Emotion: ["God (the Holy Spirit) is love, and anyone who lives in love is living with God and God is living in him"] (1 John 4:16, *Ibid.*).
[5] If you believe that Jesus is the [Messiah]—that he is God's Son and your Savior (from sin)—then you are a child of God ... because He has given (imparted) to us of His (Holy) Spirit ... so that you may know ... that you [already] have ... eternal life" (1 John 5:1, *Ibid.*; 1 John 4:13; 5:13, *Amplified Bible*).
[6] 1 Cor. 6:19, *(Living Bible)*.

41

"From this early beginning, ego displays our
in-born willfulness and hostility toward
others and toward God."

She further reminded me that even by casual
observation I could see the great hazards of
a life controlled by the human ego.[7]

It invariably leads to
   self-love
   self-seeking
   much unhappiness and tragedy.

   Human nature shows itself
     in immoral actions, witchcraft,
     hatred, strife, jealousy, wrath,
     and envy, murder and the like
     (See Gal. 5:19-20, *Good News for
     Modern Man, Living Bible*).

On the other hand,
   as we walk in the Spirit,
   and follow His leading,
   He releases and frees us.
     " 'When the Holy Spirit controls our lives
     he will produce . . . in us: love, joy, peace,
     patience, kindness, faithfulness. . . .' "[8]

The professor then opened to me
   a whole new dimension of thinking

---

[7] Self, ego, self-will, and "I" used interchangeably.
[8] Gal. 5:22 (*Living Bible*).

as she explained *how* the Spirit of God
enables us to be
 God-centered instead of self-centered.

"You must relinquish control of your life
to the Holy Spirit and live in
conscious cooperation with Him.

"Why not?" she asked. "He can do more with
your life than you can!"

I learned . . .
 it is one thing to have the Holy Spirit
 within me . . .
 and quite another to have
 Him in complete control.⁹

For example . . .
 As we board a plane, it would be unthinkable
 to say to the pilot in charge of the aircraft:

  "You take my seat.
  I'd like to sit at the controls
  and direct this flight."

How ridiculous!

 Only the skilled pilot is qualified;
 the risk would be far too great!

But is it not far more ridiculous to think we are
able to control our lives better than God, the
Holy Spirit?

---

⁹ "The Spirit has given us life; he must also control our lives" (Gal. 5:25, *Good News for Modern Man*).

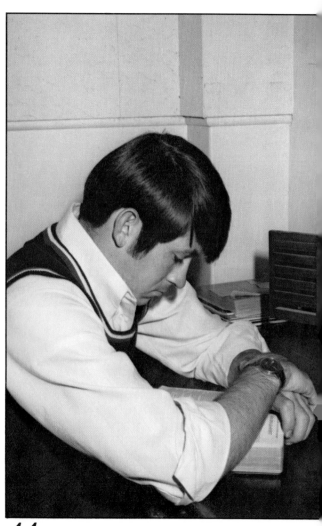

He is infinitely
   wise
   loving
   and trustworthy.
He sees the end from the beginning.

The professor then showed me what God's Word says about this imperative choice of control:

> "We naturally love to do evil things
> that are just the opposite from the things
> that the Holy Spirit tells us to do; and
> the good things we want to do when the
> Spirit has his way with us are just the
> opposite of our natural desires.
>
> "These two forces within us are constantly
> fighting each other to win control over
> us. . . . The one to whom you offer yourself—
> he will take you and be your master and
> you will be his slave. [10]

To which master did I want to give my life:
   the Holy Spirit
   or sinful self?

After seriously considering this question,
   one day, while sitting at my desk
   in the dorm,

---

[10] Gal. 5:17; Rom. 6:16b (*Ibid.*).

I simply bowed my head and said:

"Lord, I want the Holy Spirit
to take control of my life.
I step down from the control
seat and trust Him to take
over completely."

There was no dramatic manifestation or high
feeling of exultation!

However, the Holy Spirit's control produced
amazing new freedom
joy
and *direction*.
He taught me to recognize the frustrations and
pressures caused by self-will.

He gave active relief in situations when I
appealed to Him for help.

For instance—
shortly thereafter I was home for
Christmas vacation.

The entire family was enjoying the holiday
preparations until the Christmas tree ordeal!
I was unhappy and registering my complaints

46

because the tree not only looked ghastly,
but was being put in the wrong spot.

Another member of the family commented
forcefully:

> "What's wrong with putting it in front
> of the window again? The tree looked
> great there last year."

What was I to do . . .
> demand my way about the tree
> or yield the right-of-way to another?

"Why did it matter where the tree was placed?"
you may ask.

But it was far more than that! Many serious
conflicts in my home began with just such a
simple argument that climaxed in
anger and insults.[11]

At this particular time of conflict over the
Christmas tree, the Holy Spirit brought to
my mind:

> "Love does not demand its own way.
> It is not irritable or touchy."[12]

---

[11] "Now you must get rid of . . . anger . . . hateful feelings
. . . insults . . . [because] you have put off the old self . . . and
have put on the new self . . . which God . . . is constantly re-
newing in his own image . . ." (Col. 3:8-10, *Good News for
Modern Man*).

[12] 1 Cor. 13:5 *(Living Bible)*.

But I was irritable and demanding my own way!

In distress, I turned to my strong Friend for help.[13]

> "Forgive me, Lord. Please take over
> and give me Your love. Don't let me
> spoil our short time together. Not my
> will, but Yours."

He responded to this call,
    changed my attitude,
    and restored harmony in our home.

> "For God is at work within you,
>   helping you want to obey him, and
>   then helping you do what he wants."[14]

Many times, however, self has risen up and
grabbed the controls! I have temporarily
demanded my own way . . .
    told God to get off my back . . .
    let me enjoy being mean
    and doing what I want.

But soon I realize my selfish way is phony and
inferior to His plan for my life.

---

[13] "In my distress I called upon the Lord . . . he heard my
voice . . . and my cry came before him, even into his ears"
(Ps. 18:6, *King James Version*).

[14] Phil. 2:13 (*Living Bible*).

I am miserable until I confess my willfulness,
  ask the Lord to forgive me
  and to take control again.[15]

Then He restores the joy of our friendship
  and gives the quiet assurance that even
  through my times of rebellion and defeat,
    as in times of obedience and triumph,
    He never rejects me or stops loving me.[16]

  "My God is changeless in his love
  for me and he will come and help
  me."[17]

  "For God has said, 'I will never,
  never fail you nor forsake you.' "[18]

(to page 52)

---

[15] "If we are living in the light of God's presence . . . then we have wonderful fellowship and joy with each other, and the blood of Jesus his Son cleanses us from every sin [and guilt]" (1 John 1:7, *Living Bible*).

[16] "Even when we are too weak to have any faith left, he remains faithful to us and will help us, for he cannot disown us who are part of himself, and he will always carry out his promises to us" (2 Tim. 2:13, *Ibid.*).

[17] Ps. 59:10 *(Ibid.)*.

[18] Heb. 13:5 *(Living Bible)*.

Lord, life was confusing.
I tried in my own strength—
Yes, I really tried.
And it never seemed
quite right, quite complete.
I knew You were the answer,
and I had You—all of You—
in the person of the Holy Spirit.
But He didn't have all of me.
It all seems so clear now.
You want me—to fill and control me;
To renew my life in Your likeness;
You want me—not what I can do for You.
Strange that I ever thought
I could help You—the God of the universe.
If You don't do Your work through me,
it won't last—it will profit nothing.
When weighed on Your scales,
it won't stand the test of eternity.
It's not my works, You said,
or I would surely boast.
It's You working through me,
and that's far better—easier, for sure.
Then You receive all the glory, Lord,
for it belongs to You—
the glory belongs to You—
Now and for eternity!

M. J. J.

The Spirit of God increasingly made
me aware of
God's greatest interest . . .
   sharing His Son with everyone as
   the only way to an abundant life.[19]

Christ's inexpressible love for me—and
the world—became so real that it made
me willing for God to help Himself to
   my life
   my time
   and my resources.

The urgency of sharing Jesus Christ
became my top priority, making total
involvement for Him a joy and
privilege.

I could not withhold from others what would
mean life or death to them.

Life is so complete as I experience the Holy
Spirit's control and the joy He gives in sharing

---

[19] "Then said Jesus unto them again . . . I am come that
they might have life, and that they might have it more
abundantly" (John 10:7, 10, *King James Version*).

Christ with others, that my heart knows
  For this I was born!

Yes, God's living Word, empowered by the Holy Spirit, is the only accurate source of truth and **direction**—and our only hope in a confused world.

**GOD
the FATHER created me for
LOVE**

**GOD
the SON redeemed me for
LOVE**

**GOD
the HOLY SPIRIT empowers me for
LOVE**

—*Cecil Osborne*

Thank You, Lord, for opening
the eyes of my soul,
And moving my will to
want Your will—completely.
Thank You—it's so different now.
Amazing how we hold back,
afraid of perfect love,
or simply reject it.
Forgive me, Lord—
I thought more of my own
interests than Yours.
I trusted others and things
more than You.
Thank You for the person You
used to enlighten my understanding,
to make it all reasonable to me.
I could have drifted on in
mediocrity, enjoying good things,
but missing out on Your best.
If someone had not been faithful
and prayed—and believed.

M. J. J.

"The Holy Spirit is not a substitute for Jesus. The Holy Spirit is all that Jesus was, made real in personal experience now."
—*Oswald Chambers*

I Know Where I'm Goin'

R.D. & M.H.

Ray Dahrouge
and Mickey Holiday

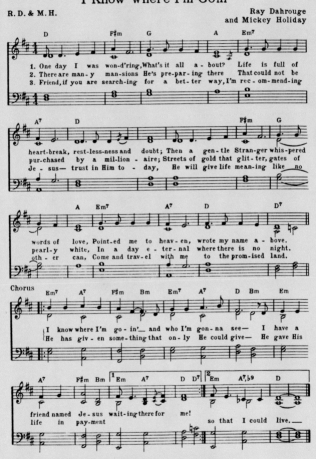

1. One day I was won-d'ring, What's it all a-bout? Life is full of
2. There are man-y man-sions He's pre-par-ing there That could not be
3. Friend, if you are search-ing for a bet-ter way, I'm rec-om-mend-ing

heart-break, rest-less-ness and doubt; Then a gen-tle Stran-ger whis-pered
pur-chased by a mil-lion-aire; Streets of gold that glit-ter, gates of
Je - sus— trust in Him to - day, He will give life mean-ing like no

words of love, Point-ed me to heav-en, wrote my name a-bove.
pearl-y white, In a day e-ter-nal where there is no night.
oth-er can, Come and trav-el with me to the prom-ised land.

Chorus

I know where I'm go-in'— and who I'm gon-na see— I have a
He has giv-en some-thing that on-ly He could give— He gave His

friend named Je-sus wait-ing there for me!
life in pay-ment so that I could live.—

Motivation

Lord, You said,
"Behold, I am the God
of all flesh.
Is there anything
too hard for me?"*
I tremble when You direct
that question my way,
for You live in me.
My inner being
is Christ's home.
Why am I ever weak
when I can have Your strength?
Why should I fear
when You say,
"I am with you always."**
I would hide myself in You.
No longer I—but Christ;
No longer I—dear Lord!

—M. J. J.

*Jer. 32:27   **Matt. 28:20

A noted engineering executive stated recently,

"With company mergers
and political maneuvering,
my life's ideals and accomplishments
are being challenged and cut down.

"This leaves me with the alternatives of
working under very adverse circumstances,
leaving the company,
or taking early retirement from the projects
I've enjoyed and lived to build.

"How can I have daily motivation to cope with this situation?"

On a college campus, a gifted coed reflected,

"Life's a drag most of the time.
You get 'turned on,'
then feel like crawling the walls
or 'flaking out.'
Guess you might as well check out now
as thirty years from now.
Seems pretty hopeless to me."

Recently, in one year alone, an estimated 25,000 people in the United States committed suicide.

Another 200,000 attempted suicide, of which
a great number were college students.[1]

How perplexing that we should be
   bored with our blessings
   pressured to escapisms
   and unchallenged in the midst of
   unparalleled opportunities.

What makes multitudes cry,
   "Stop the world, I want to get off"?

Why are millions hoping that
   alcohol
   drugs
   sexual experiences
   and materialism
   will give them satisfaction?

What is the motivating dynamic that will
   captivate and mobilize the young . . .
   revitalize and challenge the over-forty . . .
   sustain and fulfill the older members
      of society . . .
   as they contemplate moving into eternity,
   their permanent residence?

(to page 69)

---

[1] Dr. Armond Nicholi, Harvard University, Laymen's Institute, Houston, Texas.

We stumble on
and do not understand,
We only see
the future bigly planned
And watch the tapering
paths of our own mind,
And in each other's
dearest ways we stand,
And hiss and hate
And the blind
fight the blind.

—*Captain Sorley*

Moreover, confronted as we are daily with
   responsibilities
   frustrations
   hang-ups
   deadlines
   and disappointments,
Is there a source of power adequate to meet
these universal and personal demands?

I found the answer in the Apostle Paul's
monumental declaration on motivation:
   "I have strength for all things in Christ
   Who empowers me—I am ready for anything
   and equal to anything through Him Who
   infuses inner strength into me."[2]

Research shows that Paul wrote this after he had
   known incredible physical suffering and pain,
   endured beatings and mobbings,
   been imprisoned,
   and faced death again and again.[3]

Beyond this, he experienced the mental
anguish that came from learning his
trusted friends were being deceived and
turned against him.[4]

---

[2] Phil. 4:13 (_Amplified Bible_).
[3] 2 Cor. 11:23-31 (_Living Bible_).
[4] Gal. 4:14-20 (_Ibid._).

The work which had been established at such
great personal expenditure and sacrifice
was being undermined.

Throughout these desperate and trying circumstances, Paul manifested a
   supernatural strength
   and endurance . . .
   plus an unswerving drive to
   press on . . .
   because of his consuming desire
   to share the Living Christ with others.

Paul found his strength and motivation

    in Christ who empowered him!

When Paul encountered Jesus Christ
and turned unreservedly to Him as Savior,
   he experienced that

      "... with the heart a person believes
      (... *trusts* in and relies on Christ) and
      so is ... (declared ... acceptable to God) .... [5]

---

[5] Rom. 10:10 *(Amplified Bible)*.

70

For in Christ . . . our sins are forgiven
through the shedding of his blood."[6]

---

[6] Eph. 1:7 *(New English Bible).*

71

Having received Christ as his Messiah and Lord, Paul joyfully proclaimed:

> *In Christ*
> I have strength for all things.
> I am ready for anything.
> I am equal to anything.

Motivated by the living Christ within him,
Paul could live no longer to and for himself.*
He was impelled by the love of Christ to
live for God and communicate His message
of reconciliation to people everywhere.

His personal identification with Christ became so complete that he could say:

> ". . . I . . . consider that I died on the
> cross with Christ. And my
> present life is not that of the
> old 'I,' but the living *Christ*
> *within me. . . .*"[7]

---

* (Christ) died for all so that all those who live might live no longer to and for themselves, but to and for him who died and was raised again for their sake" (2 Cor. 5:15, *Amplified*).

[7] Gal. 2:20 (*New Testament in Modern English*, J. B. Phillips).

The apostle reached the ultimate in human experience when he could say:

> "For me to live is Christ,
> and to die is gain."[8]

> Why? How?
> Death gives me more of Christ.
> I will see Him—be with Him
> face to face.*
> Absent from this body,
> "At home with the Lord."[9]

> Forever and ever.
> Hallelujah!

That which produced this anticipation and motivation in Paul's life, as it will in ours, was his personal *knowledge* of Christ and personal *faith* in Christ.

---

* "For this world is not our home; we are looking forward to our everlasting home in heaven [with] our Savior the Lord Jesus Christ" (Heb. 13:14; Phil. 3:20, *Living Bible*).

[8] Phil. 1:21 *(King James Version)*.

[9] 2 Cor. 5:8 *(Living Bible)*.

Knowledge—learning from God's Word—the Bible—how to know Christ and His plan for our lives.

How to know Christ . . .
"He is always kind
and loving to me.[10]
faithfulness is (His) very character.[11]
[All] Truth is . . . embodied and personified in Him.[12]

His every word is a treasure of knowledge and understanding."[13]

How to know His plan for our life . . .
"He shows how to distinguish right from wrong, how to find the right decision every time.[14] For we are God's handiwork, created in Christ Jesus to devote ourselves to the good deeds for which God has designed us."[15]

---

[10] Ps. 144:2 *(Living Bible)*.
[11] Ps. 89:8 *(Ibid.)*.
[12] Eph. 4:21 *(Amplified Bible)*.
[13] Prov. 2:6 *(Living Bible)*.
[14] Prov. 2:9 *(Ibid.)*.
[15] Eph. 2:10 *(New English Bible)*.

Faith—reaching out and taking from Christ
what He has promised to give us
and do through us.

> Jesus said, "Yes, ask anything using
> my name, and I will do it."[16]
> "And we are sure of this, that he will
> listen to us whenever we ask him for
> anything in line with his will. And . . .
> we can be sure that he will answer us."[17]

God's provision is available through *prayer* . . .
His personal way of giving us all we need
out of His abundant riches.
Take . . . God loves you!

> "That out of His glorious, unlimited
> resources he will give you the mighty
> inner strengthening of his Holy Spirit
> . . . who by his mighty power at work
> within us is able to do far more than
> we would ever dare to ask or even dream of—
> infinitely beyond our highest prayers,
> desires, thoughts, or hopes."[18]

With promises like these, can you think of anything He cannot do?

---

[16] John 14:14 *(Living Bible)*.
[17] 1 John 5:14-15 *(Ibid.)*.
[18] Eph. 3:16, 20 *(Ibid.)*.

75

History proves that through *ordinary* people
   He subdued corruption,
   did the miraculous,
   and changed the course of individuals,
     homes,
      and nations.

A delightful homemaker related to me
how she experienced God's resources
and motivating power during a family crisis.

"Recently, our son received his summons
for the armed service.

"The day before he was to leave, it really
got to me. I felt depressed and apprehensive.

"That morning, my husband and I made plans
for a pleasant early dinner. The family
would spend the last evening together.
"I occupied the day preparing the meal our
son liked best. I prayed, but felt overpowered
in my loneliness.

" 'Oh, Lord, You've promised that I'm
to have strength for all things in Christ
who empowers me—that I'm to be equal
to anything as You infuse inner strength
into me.

" 'I want our son to see Your strength in me—
and to experience it, too. Please take over.'

"And, wonderfully, *He did!* His very
present help gave comfort and peace right
there in the kitchen.[19]

"Dinner was ready.
All the family was home—
all except Dad!
"Six o'clock came . . .
six-thirty . . .
seven. . . .

"We made the best of having dinner without
him, but I was feeling the increased strain.
Many times throughout that evening, I
quietly repeated, 'I have strength for all
things.'

"Later, my son went out to say good-by to
those he had not seen during the day.

"About midnight, I heard a commotion.
I looked from our bedroom balcony
and could see our son helping his
father up the stairs. In his drunkenness, he
couldn't make it on his own.

(to page 79)

---

[19] "He will keep in perfect peace all those who trust in
him, whose thoughts turn often to the Lord" (Isa. 26:3,
Ibid.).

77

It is in times of calamity,
in days and nights of sorrow
    and trouble,
that the Presence,
the sufficiency,
and the sympathy of God
    grow very sure
and very wonderful.
Then we find out
that the grace of God
is sufficient for
    all our needs,
for every problem . . .
for every difficulty . . .
for every broken heart . . .
and for every human sorrow.

—*Peter Marshall*

"Concern,
   fear,
   anger,
   and self-pity overwhelmed me.

" 'I'm coming unglued.' I thought, as my knees turned to rubber. 'How could he do this to us —tonight of all times! This will be our son's last memory of home.'
"Then, suddenly and spontaneously, I was reminded of those words of strength and comfort:

   " 'I am ready for anything and equal
   to anything through Him Who infuses
   inner strength into me.'[20]

"God's promise in Isaiah 41:13 also flashed into my mind:

   " 'I am holding you by your right
   hand—I, the Lord your God—and
   I say to you, Don't be afraid; I
   am here to help you' *(Living Bible)*.

" 'Oh, Lord, I almost forgot! You are here! I need Your strength. We all need it. And now I take it.'

---

[20] Phil. 4:13 *(Amplified Bible)*.

"And strengthen us He did. Silently and quickly, He came to our rescue—and kept my mouth shut!

"I helped our son put his father to bed, and later I lay praying and thanking the Lord that as He had undertaken in us that day, so He would be with us tomorrow.

"I knew the Lord loved my husband just as he was—and wanted to give him a new life. 'Please help him to want it,' I prayed.

"He was in no condition to arise at 4:30 a.m. and go with us to the station, but again we received new strength.

" 'As thy days, so shall thy strength be.'[21]

"Yes, I had strength . . .
His strength in my utter weakness.
Strength to smile and to be confident as we waved good-by.
Strength to return home and face the working out of our problems there."[22]

---

[21] Deut. 33:25 *(King James Version).*

[22] "God who gives you hope will keep you happy and full of peace as you believe in him. I pray that God will help you overflow with hope in him through the Holy Spirit's power within you" (Rom. 15:13, *Living Bible).*

What *motivation!*

What *reality!*

Today, we marvel at the modern wonder of
sending men to the moon.

> But the greater wonder is
> God sending His Son to earth
> to redeem us,
> Having Him come to make His
> home in our lives,
> And *now* making available to us
> the same supernatural power for
> motivation that He possessed.

Will we take and use His provision?

**What impact does Jesus Christ have
in and through your life?**

"To all who received him, he gave the right to become children of God. All they needed to do was to trust [Christ] to save them. All those who believe this are reborn!" (John 1:12-13, *Living Bible*).

"And he is able to keep you from slipping and falling away, to bring you . . . into his glorious presence with mighty shouts of everlasting joy" (Jude 25, *Living Bible*).

MY PERSONAL COMMITMENT

Suggested prayer:

Dear God, I realize there is no rerun on life and no substitute for personally knowing Your Son, Jesus Christ. I've sinned against You and others in thought, word, and deed. I need and want Your forgiveness.

Thank You, Lord and Savior, for taking the cruel punishment for my sins. Please come into my life and cleanse me.

Free me from attitudes which bind me; change my evil desires; give me the strength to follow You completely. Take control of my will and guide me day by day according to Your plan.

I now commit myself to You, Lord Jesus, believing You have the power to keep me through all the circumstances of life until You take me to be with You forever.

Thank You, Father, for giving me Your Holy Spirit and eternal life through Your Son. In Jesus' Name. Amen.

Signed ....

Date ....

Yesterday, Today and Tomorrow

Jack Wyrtzen

Don Wyrtzen

May be simplified for guitar by playing all four stanzas in the key of D (third stanza), sustaining the D chord at the end of the stanza instead of modulating through the Bb7 chord at the end.

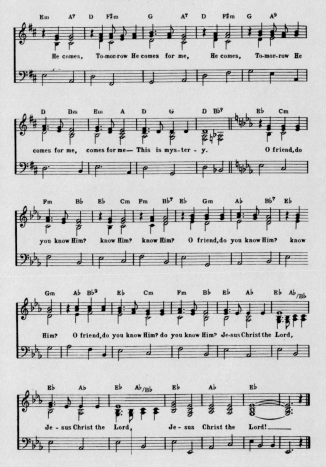

Lord, how truly great
that You are so available!
Your resources are infinite
and You are never
the poorer for giving.
Thank You for the reminder
'You have not because you ask not.'
Forgive us for being small people
and not representing You clearly.
Thank You for Your patience
and the constant encouragement
from Your Word.
I'd like to share it
with someone today.
I'm available!

M. J. J.

Spiritual Fitness

This is the beginning of a new day. God has given me this day to use as I will. I can waste it—or use it for good, but what I do today is important, because I am exchanging a day of my life for it! When tomorrow comes, this day will be gone forever, leaving in its place something that I have traded for it. I want it to be gain, and not loss; good, and not evil; success, and not failure; in order that I shall not regret the price that I have paid for it.

Dr. Heartsill Wilson

"Spend your time and energy
in the exercise of keeping
spiritually fit.
Bodily exercise is all right,
but spiritual exercise
is much more important
and is a tonic
for all you do.
So exercise yourself
spiritually
and practice being
a better Christian,
because that will help you
not only now in this life,
but in the next life too.*

—*The Bible*

---

* 1Tim. 4:7-8 *(Living Bible)*.

I have found the following steps to Spiritual Fitness most essential and rewarding: (1) Eat Well (2) Trust—Rest (3) Communicate (4) Exercise.

EAT WELL

Reading the Bible daily and meditating on it is God's personal way of nourishing you spiritually. The Holy Spirit will make the Bible come alive as you ask Him to move the words from the page into your life.

> "Eat God's Word—read it, think about it— and grow strong in the Lord."[1]

> "Man shall not live and be upheld and sustained by bread alone, but by every word that comes forth from the mouth of God."[2]

> "I assure you (Jesus said) . . . the person whose ears are open to My word—who . . . believes . . . and relies on Him Who sent Me has (possesses now) eternal life."[3]

The *Psalms* teach you how to *pray* and the *Proverbs* teach you how to *live*. By reading five Psalms

---

[1] 1 Pet. 2:3 *(author's paraphrase).*
[2] Matt. 4:4 *(Ibid.)*
[3] John 5:24 *(Ibid.).*

and one chapter of Proverbs daily, you can read through the Psalms and Proverbs each month. You will discover that these relevant words have life and voice.

> "... in a humble, (gentle) ... spirit receive and welcome the Word (of God) ... obey the message. Carry out my instructions; don't forget them, for they will lead you to real living."[4]

> "... thank God that when you received ... the Word of God's message, you accepted it not as the word of men, but for what it really is, the word of God, which also performs its work in you who believe."[5]

Begin reading the Gospel by Dr. Luke. Underline the thoughts meaningful to you. Review at night. Increase intake as appetite increases. Follow this procedure with other books of the Bible.

> "Your words are what sustain me; they are food to my hungry soul. They bring joy to my sorrowing heart and delight me. ... They are my constant guide."[6]

---

[4] James 1:21-22 *(Ibid.)*; Prov. 4:13 *(Living Bible)*.
[5] 1 Thess. 2:13 *(New American Standard Bible)*.
[6] Jer. 15:16; Ps. 119:98 *(Living Bible)*.

Break Thou the Bread of Life

MARY A. LATHBURY   WILLIAM F. SHERWIN

1. Break Thou the bread of life, Dear Lord, to me, As Thou didst
2. Bless Thou the truth, dear Lord, To me— to me— As Thou didst
3. Thou art the bread of life, O Lord, to me, Thy ho - ly
4. O send Thy Spir - it, Lord, Now un - to me, That He may

break the loaves Be - side the sea; Be - yond the sa - cred page
bless the bread By Gal - i - lee; Then shall all bond-age cease,
Word the truth That sav - eth me; Give me to eat and live
touch my eyes, And make me see: Show me the truth con-cealed

I seek Thee, Lord; My spir - it pants for Thee, O liv - ing Word.
All fet - ters fall; And I shall find my peace, My All in all.
With Thee a - bove; Teach me to love Thy truth, For Thou art love.
With - in Thy Word, And in Thy book re-vealed I see the Lord.

"... your promises ... give me strength in all my troubles; how they refresh and revive me!"[7]

**"Jesus said ...
I am the bread of life:
he that cometh to me shall never hunger. ...
The words
that I speak unto you,
they are spirit,
and they are life."**[8]

Eating adequate portions of God's Word and meditating on it gives you spiritual strength and vitality for each day. There is no substitute for the Bread of Life!

"I will quietly keep my mind upon your promises. Nothing is perfect except your words. Oh, how I love them. Your words are a flashlight to light the path ahead of me, and keep me from stumbling. Your Word has been my comfort ... my source of joy and singing."

King David   *(to page 103)*

---

[7] Ps. 119:49-50 *(Ibid.)*.
[8] John 6:35, 63 *(King James Version)*.

I love You Lord,
not doubtingly,
but with absolute certainty.
Your Word beat upon my heart
until I fell in love with You,
and now the universe
and everything in it
tells me to love You
and tells the same things
to us all so that
we are without excuse.

Saint Augustine

Speak, Lord, in the Stillness

QUIET HOUR

E. MAY GRIMES, 1868-1927

Source unknown
Arr. by Alfred B. Smith, 1916-

1. Speak, Lord, in the still - ness, While I wait on Thee;
2. Speak, O bless - ed Mas - ter, In this qui - et hour;
3. For the words Thou speak - est, They are life in - deed;
4. All to Thee is yield - ed— I am not my own!
5. Fill me with the knowl - edge Of Thy glo - rious will;
6. Like a wa - tered gar - den Full of fra - grance rare,

Hush'd my heart to lis - ten, In ex - pect - an - cy.
Let me see Thy face, Lord, Feel Thy touch of pow'r.
Liv - ing Bread from heav - en, Now my spir - it feed!
Bliss - ful, glad sur - ren - der— I am Thine a - lone!
All Thine own good plea - sure In Thy child ful - fill.
Lin - g'ring in Thy pres - ence, Let my life ap - pear.

Once I had misgivings
   about You and
   Your Word, Lord.
Once I found it hard
to trust and not doubt.
But day by day
You've proven Your
Love and promises to me
   in such a way,
   in so many ways, Lord,
I find it harder now
to doubt than *trust*.

M. J. J.

"Your faith can only be as great as the Person
you trust."

TRUST—REST

Trust, rely on, *rest,* and relax in the promises God gives you from His Word each day. When a promise meets a special need, write it on a card and read it during the day. Memorize it.

Thank God that His Spirit lives in you and is working all things together for your good.
> "And we know that all that happens to us is working for our good if we love God and are fitting into his plans."[9]

> "*Trust* in the Lord with all thine heart; and lean not unto thine own understanding. In all thy ways acknowledge him, and he shall direct thy paths."[10]

> "In everything give thanks; for this is the will of God in Christ Jesus concerning you."[11]

Learn to *commit* (hand over, release) your duties, problems, frustrations, and people to the Lord. He frees you from futile self-effort.

> "Commit everything you do to the Lord. Trust him to help you do it and he will. . . . then it will succeed."[12]

---

[9] Rom. 8:28 *(Living Bible).*
[10] Prov. 3:5-6 *(King James Version).*
[11] 1 Thess. 5:18 *(Ibid.).*
[12] Ps. 37:5; Prov. 16:3 *(Living Bible).*

"But as for me . . . I would commit my cause
to God, who does great and unsearchable
things, marvelous works without number."[13]

---

[13] Job 5:8 *(New Berkeley Version in Modern English).*

Learn to *rest* and be quiet inwardly by trusting God to act on your behalf. "Do not let happy trust in the Lord die away, no matter what happens."

"Lord, when doubts fill my mind, when my heart is in turmoil, quiet me and give me renewed hope and cheer."[14]

"Rest in the Lord; wait patiently for him to act.... Stop your anger! ... Don't fret and worry—it only leads to harm." [15]

"And the Lord said, My presence shall go with you, and I will give you *rest*. ... His peace will keep your thoughts and your hearts quiet and at rest as you trust in Christ Jesus."[16]

This spiritual therapy relaxes you and gives confidence and poise. It helps to create a buoyant mental attitude; moreover, it provides fresh courage and motivation.

(to page 108)

---

[14] Heb. 10:35; Ps. 94:19 *(Living Bible)*.

[15] Ps. 37:7-8 *(Ibid.)*.

[16] Exod. 3:14 *(Amplified Bible)*; 1 Pet. 1:21 *(Living Bible)*; Phil. 4:7 *(Ibid.)*.

There is a strength
That comes through prayer,
A confidence, a power,
A quiet, deep, unflinching faith
To meet the trying hour.

There is a peace
That comes through prayer,
A calm serenity
To face whatever life may hold
With grace and dignity.

There is a joy
That comes through prayer,
A gladness of the soul,
A glorious sense of having been
Refreshed, renewed, made whole.

Helen Lowrie Marshall

"Speaking with God discovers us safely to ourselves. We find ourselves, come to ourselves, as we learn to pray in the power of the Holy Spirit."

Peter Taylor Forsyth

COMMUNICATE

Enjoy your friendship with the Lord! He loves you! In turn, express your love, worship, and appreciation to Him.

"O Lord, you are worthy to receive the glory and the honor and the power, for you have created all things. With all my heart I [love and] will praise you.... for you love me so much. You are merciful and gentle... full of constant lovingkindness and of truth."[17]

It helps to talk with a Friend. The Lord is understanding and does not break confidence. Don't be afraid to communicate with Him.

"I love the Lord because he hears my prayers and answers them... he bends down and listens...."[18]

Ask Him to forgive your sins, neglect, and failures.

"But if **we** confess our sins to him, he can be **depended** on to forgive us and to cleanse us from **every** wrong... because Christ died to wash away our sins."[19]

---

[17] Rev. 4:11; Ps. 12-13, 15 (*Living Bible*).
[18] Ps. 116:1-2 (*Ibid.*).
[19] 1 John 1:9 (*Ibid.*).

Talk with Him about your family, friends, and relatives. Ask Him to give you His love for them and everyone.

> "... how I need your help, especially in my own home, where I long to act as I should. ... for we know how dearly God loves us, and we feel this warm love everywhere within us because God has given us the Holy Spirit to fill our hearts with his love."[20]

Talk with Him about your personality problems, passions, and fears.

> "In my distress I prayed to the Lord and he answered me and rescued me. He is for me! How can I be afraid? What can mere man do to me? ... Though I am surrounded by troubles, you will bring me safely through them."[21]

Talk with Him about your health, finances, and business propositions.

> "When I pray, you answer me, and encourage me by giving me the strength I need. ... The Lord will work out his plans for my life (and business). ... Don't worry about anything;

---

[20] Ps. 101:2; Rom. 5:5 *(Ibid.).*
[21] Pss. 118:5-6; 138:7 *(Ibid.).*

instead, pray about everything; tell God your needs and don't forget to thank him for his answers."[22]

Ask Him to comfort and help those you know who are struggling, suffering, and dying.

"When you go through deep waters and great trouble . . . difficulty . . . oppression . . . yes, . . . the valley of the shadow of death. . . . Don't be afraid. . . . I will be with you. . . . You are mine . . . and I love you."[23]

Talk with Him about your neighbors, community, state, nation, and world.

". . . Pray much for others . . . for . . . all . . . who are in authority over us . . . in . . . high responsibility . . . . give thanks for all he is going to do for them. . . . for he longs for all to be saved and to understand [the] truth."[24]

Your prayer involvement takes on new perspective, priority, and praise when you learn the Lord hears, cares, and answers. "Pray without a break between your prayer and your life."[25]

(to page 113)

---

[22] Ps. 138:3, 8; Phil. 4:6 *(Ibid.)*.
[23] Isa. 43:1-5 *(Ibid.)*; Ps. 23:4; Isa. 43:5 *(New Berkeley Version)*.
[24] 1 Tim. 2:1-2, 4 *(Living Bible)*.
[25] *Soul of Prayer*, P. T. Forsyth.

O Christ, our living Lord, Thou hast brought us to this new day and further opportunity.

Help us to work with Thee that it may be a good day with good things done. We know that a "different world cannot be built by indifferent people."

Abide with us, O Christ, that our hearts may burn within us and our imaginations be fired with Thy passion to do God's will. Amen.

Peter Marshall

EXERCISE

Get up—out—share with others. God wants to make each day count.

"I . . . will make the hours of your day more profitable and the years of your life more fruitful."
"Teach us to number our days and recognize how few they are; help us to spend them as we should."[26]

Whenever possible, plan your routine activities. Ask the Lord to give you His joy in doing them.

"We should make plans—counting on God to direct us."[27]

"Satisfy us in our earliest youth with your lovingkindness, giving us constant joy to the end of our lives."[28]

Don't be afraid to get involved. Ask Him to give you an outreach where you can exercise your talents and abilities in helping others.

"God has given each of you some special abilities; be sure to use them to help each other. . . ."[29]

---

26 Prov. 9:11; Ps. 90:12 *(Living Bible).*
27 Prov. 16:9 *(Ibid.).*
28 Ps. 90:14 *(Ibid.).*
29 1 Pet. 4:10 *(Living Bible).*

". . . Be strong and courageous and get to work. Don't be frightened by the size of the task, for the Lord my God is with you; he will not forsake you. He will see to it that everything is finished correctly."[30]

Give and accept forgiveness.

"Be gentle and ready to forgive; never hold grudges. Remember, the Lord forgave you, so you must forgive others."[31]

Permit the Lord to show His love through you.

"Most important of all, continue to show deep love for each other, for love makes up for many of your faults . . . . love overlooks insults. . . . Love forgets mistakes. Now you can have real love for everyone because [of] the great love for others which the Holy Spirit has given you."[32]

Exercise sharing the Person of Christ by introducing Him to others.

"(He) came that they may have and enjoy life, and have it in abundance—to the full, till it overflows."[33]

---

[30] 1 Chron. 28:20 *(Ibid.).*
[31] Col. 3:13 *(Ibid.).*
[32] 1 Pet. 4:8; Prov. 10:12; 17:9; 1 Pet. 1:22; Col. 1:8 *(Ibid.).*
[33] John 10:10 *(Amplified Bible).*

"For I am not ashamed of this Good News about Christ. It is God's powerful method of bringing all who believe it to heaven. . . ."[34]

"Go home to your (family and) friends . . . and tell them what wonderful things God has done for you. . . ."[35]

The greatest thing a human being can do is to bring another human being to Jesus Christ.

> I thank You, Lord, for my friend,
> I pray that he may come to know You
> through Jesus Christ our Lord.
> I pray that in my friendship with him
> I may be Your servant.
> Show me when to speak and how to speak.
> Show me also when to be silent.
> And I pray that the Holy Spirit,
> who found a way to turn me round and
> find life,
> may also work the same great work
> in him.
>
> —*Dick Williams*

---

[34] Rom. 1:16 (*Living Bible*).
[35] Mark 5:19 (*Ibid.*).

The consistent practice of this Spiritual Fitness Plan develops a natural reflex that makes you aware of God's friendship twenty-four hours a day. It increases your ability to perform daily duties adequately with His resources to meet any emergency.

The exciting and fulfilling result is that we can function at maximum capacity according to God's plan and *enjoy* it. Life really has meaning! Try it and see for yourself.

"Stay in happy
fellowship with the Lord
so that when he comes
you will be sure
that all is well,
and will not have to be
ashamed and shrink back
from meeting him."*

The Bible

---

* 1 John 2:28 *(Living Bible).*

Happiness Is the Lord

I. F. S.

Ira F. Stanphill

1. Hap-pi-ness is to know the Sav-ior, Liv-ing a life with-in His fa-vor,
2. Hap-pi-ness is a new cre - a - tion—"Je-sus and me" in close re - la - tion,
3. Hap-pi-ness is to be for-giv-en, Liv-ing a life that's worth the liv-in',

Hav-ing a change in my be-hav-ior— Hap-pi-ness is the Lord;
Hav-ing a part in His sal-va-tion—
Tak-ing a trip that leads to heav-en—

Hap-pi-ness is the Lord. Real joy is mine, no mat-ter if tear-drops start; I've

found the se-cret—it's Je-sus in my heart! Hap-pi-ness is the

Lord, Hap-pi-ness is the Lord, Hap-pi-ness is the Lord!